October Guests

fal

First edition 2009

© Caroline Carver, Victoria Field, Penelope Shuttle
Cover photographs: Victoria Field
All rights reserved

ISBN 978-0-9555661-1-0

published by

fal publications
PO Box 74
Truro
TR1 1XS

www.falpublications.co.uk

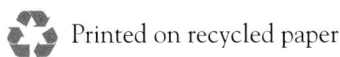 Printed on recycled paper

Printed by
R. Booth Ltd
The Praze, Penryn, Cornwall TR10 8AA

October Guests

Caroline Carver
Victoria Field
Penelope Shuttle

Contents:

Poets and Poetry in Cornwall	1
History - Just one damn thing after another	4
A year later	6
Poems and Reflections – Caroline Carver	7
Poems and Reflections – Victoria Field	11
Poems and Reflections – Penelope Shuttle	15
Acknowledgements	20

POETS AND POETRY IN CORNWALL

Penelope Shuttle

> 'The whole world's water at some time or another
> Flows through the Carrick Roads, bringing
> Its memories…'

These lines are from *Living in Falmouth*, a long poem by Peter Redgrove, who lived in Falmouth most of his life. Falmouth is a deepwater port in the far-west of Cornwall, and his poem attests to the connectedness of Cornwall with the rest of the world. Both by its maritime associations and its long history of migration by its tin-miners, an industry stretching back to Phoenician times, Cornwall has always been in touch with the rest of the world. This connectedness is also there, vitally, in its creative life. For many years, painters and writers have been drawn to Cornwall, fascinated by its light, its atmosphere, its ability to be both far from the wider world, and yet part of it.

Cornwall, long, narrow and green, is bounded by the sea on three sides; almost an island, and the quality of its light comes from the constant bouncing back and forth of light as it reflects up from sea to sky and back again and again and again…

Cornwall has a powerful un-English sense of identity. Until the 18th century Cornish, a language closer to Breton and Welsh than to English, was widely spoken and my own first impression of Cornwall, when I got off the bus at St Erth in the summer of 1969, was of this un-English-ness. The signposts to towns and villages were in another language – Degibna, Zelah, Halzephron – they were in Cornish. Every church was dedicated to saints I'd never heard of – St Mylor, St Levan, St Buryan, St Materiana – and I soon learned the Cornish saying that there are more saints in Cornwall than in heaven. As poets we are constantly reminded of the magic of this lost shadow language, Cornish.

Poetry is alive and kicking in Cornwall. In 1972, Peter Redgrove founded the Falmouth Poetry Group, and FPG continues to this day, having had subsequent Chairs: Derek Power, Michael Bayley, Jane Tozer, and, currently, myself. The group focuses on intensive workshopping of new poems by members. We have organized several poetry festivals and continue to hold readings and workshops.

Other Cornish towns, especially Liskeard, Redruth, Camelford and Penzance, have strong poetry communities. The Cornish Literary Guild focuses on traditional poets and the recently-formed Charles Causley Society celebrates this most Cornish, yet widely-travelled of poets. *Poetry Cornwall*, a magazine edited by Les Merton, is based in Redruth. Residential courses at Camelford and at Cape Cornwall run each year.

The Cornish have always looked outwards and poets from Cornwall are no exception – rooted in a richly creative and supportive environment yet cherishing our links with poets around the world. We'll bring Cornwall to you and when we return home we'll take the gift of contact with you, of new things learned, and new poems inspired.

Finally, in words from *Living in Falmouth*,

> 'Sun steers from the muddy Falmouth east
> And docks above Swanpool, the air clears,
> The sun's great hull lies above us, it is time,
> Which is a red-hot hull. The great sun-sailors
> Take liberty and stroll about the town,
> The drawing-rooms expand as they peep in,
> The hills are emerald and the cliffs sheer gold.
> Their leave is short. They one by one ascend
> The shrinking ladders of the dusk
> Into the smaller, redder, westering boat. Shall we board
> Into the night? To a man we have a ticket.'

Yes, we have tickets.

Penelope Shuttle

HISTORY – JUST ONE DAMN THING AFTER ANOTHER

Victoria Field

In April 2005 I travelled from Cornwall to Cumbria at the invitation of Geraldine Green – she was organising a workshop and a reading by Long Island poet George Wallace and assured me of an inspirational weekend. It was. On a sunny Sunday morning, she, George, Charles Johnson and I sat over boiled eggs and coffee in Geraldine and Geoff's garden, exchanging books and CDs. I gave George a CD called *Eight Voices* featuring Cornish poets, with music and production by composer and writer Tony Lamb. Within a week of his return to the US, George had reviewed the CD on several websites and broadcast some tracks on a local radio station. He was clearly someone who made things happen.

In September 2006 Apples & Snakes and Lapidus Cornwall sponsored a visit to Falmouth by George. There he made an impression on many Cornish poets and invited Penelope Shuttle and Caroline Carver to read at some of the venues he programmes in and around New York. Caroline has a long association with Canada and so the idea for a tour grew. We were fortunate to receive an Arts Council grant and sponsorship from three poetry publishers and Cornish World magazine; the tour exceeded our expectations.

In Canada we gave readings in Toronto at the Arts & Letters Club, at the Toronto Cornwall Association and in Niagara-on-the-Lake Public Library.

In the US we read in New York at The New School, the National Arts Club and the Bowery Poetry Club, on Long Island at Huntington Poetry Barn, and in Woodstock at the Colony Cafe. At Huntington we were filmed by Michael Mart for his website www.poetryvlog.com. I also gave a workshop in Poetry Therapy at the Institute for Arts in Psychotherapy in Manhattan.

Those two weeks generated new friendships, cemented old ones, led to professional exchanges and opened our hearts and minds. People have always headed West from Cornwall and in many ways North America feels closer than London. We hope there will be opportunities to welcome some of those we met to Cornwall – to be *our* October guests, enjoy dark days of autumn rain and walk some of the beautiful sodden lanes of this corner of Britain.

A YEAR LATER
Caroline Carver

A year later the New England woods still crowd my mind. New York and Toronto expand into dream cities, fantasy landscapes where poems dance on skyscrapers and sylphs disappear alluringly into parkland.

A year later the warm friendship and hospitality of everyone we met still tingles memory – the excitement and dynamism everywhere – from a pioneer wooden barn on Long Island to the wonderments of the Arts & Letters Club in Toronto and the glorious eccentricities of the Gramercy Club in New York. Nowhere else in the world, I think, would we have had the chance to read our work standing in front of an enormous Gothic birdcage, to the accompaniment of a literary raven's 'gronk'.

POEMS AND REFLECTIONS

Caroline Carver

TORONTO LAKEFRONT

Grimy cold   tossed ashore
like discarded blocks of concrete
from a disassembled bridge

gray ice is a playground for children
in a giant's world

The boardwalk
under the pounding feet of joggers
and strolling well-wrapped middle-agers

dreams of northern forests

houses near the water
smug inside their small territories
of still clean snow

remember wilderness
Iroquois making their way north
the bright-starred arc of winter

the lake itself
big as half Switzerland
pines for summer's ocean-going ships

Yachts hibernate on the small islands
It's end of day quiet.

Beyond the pack ice
foothills of water
moody as mountain goats

trip empty-handed
to and fro   to and fro
between Canada and upstate New York

PEACEABLE KINGDOM

The train cries its way through woods of secrecy and autumn
conjuring up   like mist creeping through trees
the last strands of romantic memory –

Native Americans, woodlore at their fingertips
shaking great bird head-dresses;
pilgrim children in the Peaceable Kingdom
playing with wild animals

                                                   or so it seems at dusk

in this land full of strangers   half-way between Gods and men
where forests drift ghostlike past windows
and the whistle echoes as far as the Pacific
as if we're headed there instead of New York City.

The train makes you dream of where you hadn't meant to go
and as the sun sinks among trees with their mysterious interlacing of branches
you forget bears can be sluggish and greedy   lions moody and unpredictable
wolves full of melancholy   leopards quick to take offence

and you paint a dream picture
where settlers always find a safe path through the forest
every door is always open to strangers
every welcome   deep as the tankards of the Gods

SNAPSHOTS OF NEW YORK CITY

like ladies in a Sultan's Seraglio
New York skyscrapers wear their best dresses
jewelry glittering with all the colours of water

* * * * *

the Rainbow Room has been on the 65th floor so long
it has woven magic into the carpets
old-fashioned dancing floats on rivers of sound

* * * * *

the man cross-legged under a tree in Central Park
concentrates on his book
the rest of the planet is someplace else

* * * * *

boaters row quietly through tree-lined lives
joggers know the future is reached
not only by high speed elevators

* * * * *

in March each year
elephants walk at midnight
from railyards at Queens to Madison Square Gardens

* * * * *

that first dawn I sailed into New York
the Statue of Liberty revealed herself
Queen of the Seraglio

* * * * *

POEMS AND REFLECTIONS

Victoria Field

FLIGHT

On the plane, I'm fascinated by the back
of his neck, the way it folds itself like
dough down and around his collar,
how constellations of freckles are bears
and maidens, Pleiades and Pole Stars
on the clear sky of his skin, how
a sprinkle of stubbly hair connecting ear
to complicated ear, glints gold against
the white dome of his head, that library
where he keeps his life, where words
from the book he's reading file themselves,
busy and silent in this vastness of sky.

BANTING HOUSE INN

David finds me a second blanket
makes sure the washroom's pristine.
Paul thinks London is cool, offers
to show me toronto.com,
has the computer switched on 24/7.
Brandon poaches eggs with a timer,
serves them sprinkled with parsley,
a crescent of melon. James carries
heavy cases up two flights of stairs, turns
his grimace to a smile that reaches his eyes.

All day, they fold towels, dust the many
clocks, their shorts and piercings at odds
with polished wood and the wall-papers'
many varieties of floral, in this house
of Dr Banting, discoverer of insulin,
testing its effect on himself, being,
like James, Brandon, Paul and David,
a man concerned first for the comfort of others.

NIAGARA

The edge is luminous – a green ribbon
of unearthly, unheavenly light lifts
and turns grey water into molten emerald
so the going-over's a fall and a tumble
through the best kind of brightness
before the long drop to the depths.

SQUIRRELS
Toronto

In this city, they're black, sleek as cats
and everywhere, up trees, running
round hostas in front yards, crossing
the streets in pairs, heedless of cars,
taking what they need, knowing
that in spite of today's warmth, autumn
is falling towards them, a dark blanket
muffling their words, so now they scurry,
collecting them – *nuts, nests, shuffle
of leaves, slow, sleep, snow, night* –
long dreams of next year's seeds.

POEMS AND REFLECTIONS

Penelope Shuttle

LAKE VIEW FROM A.G.'s WINDOW
Hardwood Lake, Upper Ontario

First light knocks at the window,
bundle of sticks on its back

                      Let me in

Troubled and cold,
Lake leans on the panes
                      Gimme the time of day

Restless as an October porcupine,
Sky breathes on the glass
                      Here I am

A solitary lake-side boulder,
    older than the world,
        doesn't say a word

Every turning-red leaf
along the shore whispers
                      We want to be somewhere else

But not me –
I've drunk long enough
from the strongwater cup of the past

Here by the lake is fine by me, just fine –
admiring the trees in their sheep's clothing,

the wind moving its broken chinese fan
through the waves,
one butterfly moment in time's killing jar…

SLEEPLESS SONNET
slow train from Toronto to New York

Instead of sheep, I count the 6000 Siberian swans
wintering in the waterlands of Cambridgeshire,
then number my way through the world's
stolen and unrecovered Rembrandts,
bringing my total up to 6,142 –
to this I add the miles of shelving
in the Library of Congress
(6,672) – Somewhere near Buffalo,
still wide awake at 3am,
I tot up 50 million census takers in China,
plus the 30 million Americans who believe
their phones are tapped by their own government
and by now red-eye dawn is crossing the border,
the countless stars fading, like me.

NIGHT DEPARTURE

What's more boring than baseball?
Nothing –
yet a minute after takeoff from JFK

how beautiful, looking down
at the huge golden rectangle
of The Dodge Stadium

in which Angels are practising
their homerun hosannahs,
Saints healing the multitudinous sick

Our big plane tilts, swings east,
the bright miraculous stadium
tips back out of sight

as we rise over the vast unbending lines
of traffic fizzing with purpose,
lit-up patterns of simple practicality –

then, a rapid slideaway
over the jewelled coastline unfurling
its brilliant surf –

and into darkness
but for the now and then
glowworm of a container ship far below,

and the stars, of course,
doing their best to be as bright as NYC.

TIDY
written at Aero's Farm

I put everything back
in its rightful place –

sun and moon in the sky,
leaves back on the trees

I can't put my heart back
between my ribs –

you know why –

or return hope
to its bright little niche
in my mind

I put every raindrop
back into the cloud,

count every colour back
into the rainbow

But I'll never repair
the shattered mosaic
of our past

– lovely wild fragments –
or mend the broken mirror
of the present

even with my willing hands,
these broken hands

Acknowledgements

Caroline Carver, Penelope Shuttle and Victoria Field would like to thank the following organisations who made the tour possible:

Arts Council England
Bloodaxe Books
Cornish World
Fal Publications
Peterloo Poets
Poetry pf

and the following individuals who were so generous with their friendship and hospitality:

Jeanne Beaumont, Frank Beck, Patricia Carlin,
Gordon Chaplin, Philip Fried, Greg Gatenby,
Andy Gemmell, Geraldine Green,
Jamie & Virginia Mainprize, Stuart & Gilly Marwick,
John & Prim Pemberton, Sherry Reiter,
Ted & Jane Stephenson, Tom Stock, Monica Tross,
John Tyacke, George Wallace, Lila Weisberger,
Rex Williams

For up-to-date biographies and current listings, please visit www.poetrypf.co.uk